Amazing RECIPES You Can Make and Share

by Mari Bolte
illustrated by Paula Franco

CAPSTONE YOUNG READERS
a capstone imprint

Table of CONTENTS

Pack your bags for fun with the Sleepover Girls! Every Friday, Maren, Ashley, Delaney, and Willow get together for crafts, fashion, cooking, and, of course, girl talk! Read the books, get to know the girls, and dive in to this book of cool projects that are Sleepover Girl staples!

Bake a brownie pizza that will knock your friends off their feet, or serve them super smoothies. Chow down on birthday cake-flavored popcorn and dish over a plate of homemade spaghetti sauce. Snag a spoon, phone some friends, and start cooking with your very own Sleepover Club.

MEET THE SLEEPOVER GIRLS!

Willow Marie Keys

Patient and kind, Willow is a wonderful confidante and friend. (Just ask her twin, Winston!) She is also a budding artist with creativity for miles. Willow's Bohemian style suits her flower child within.

Maren Melissa Taylor

Maren is what you'd call "personality-plus"—sassy, bursting with energy, and always ready with a sharp one-liner. You'll often catch Maren wearing a hoodie over a sports tee and jeans. An only child, Maren has adopted her friends as sisters.

Ashley Francesca Maggio

Ashley is the baby of a lively Italian family. This fashionista-turned-blogger is on top of every style trend via her blog, Magstar. Vivacious and mischievous, Ashley is rarely sighted without her beloved "purse puppy," Coco.

Delaney Ann Brand

Delaney's smart, motivated, and always on the go! You'll usually spot low-maintenance Delaney in a ponytail and jeans (and don't forget her special charm bracelet, with charms to symbolize her Sleepover Girl buddies.)

Birthday Cake Corn

Willow knows that it takes brain power to come up with a great birthday bash idea. Feed your head (and your friends) with a party-packed popcorn ball.

WHAT YOU'LL NEED

2 bags of microwave popcorn

12 ounces (330 grams) white chocolate chips or vanilla almond bark

1 bag mini marshmallows

¼ cup (60 mL) butter

¾ cup (175 mL) vanilla cake mix

¼ cup (60 mL) sprinkles

lollipop sticks

cooking spray

1 Prepare microwave popcorn as directed on the package. Remove any unpopped kernels. Place in a large bowl and set aside.

2 Place the white chocolate, marshmallows, and butter in a microwave-safe bowl. Melt for 30 seconds in the microwave. Stir with a rubber scraper. Microwave again for 30 seconds and stir again. Continue this process until chocolate and marshmallows are completely melted.

3 Stir in the cake mix and sprinkles. Mix until everything is well combined.

4 Pour the white chocolate-sprinkle mix over the popcorn. Stir until all the popcorn is coated.

5 Spray your hands with cooking spray. Then shape the popcorn into balls.

6 Decorate balls with extra sprinkles. Push a lollipop stick into each ball. Serve in baking cups or cupcake liners.

Prickly Pear Fruit *Leather*

The Prickly Pair, Franny and Zoey, like to eat ultra-healthy the morning after a sleepover. Have this handy, homemade fruit leather ready for just such an occasion.

WHAT YOU'LL NEED

2 cups (480 mL) pear-flavored applesauce

1 cup (240 mL) blueberry-flavored applesauce

sweetener, such as sugar or honey (optional)

cooking spray

1 Taste the applesauces to make sure they're to your liking. If they're not sweet enough, stir in a little sugar or honey.

2 Turn your oven to the "warm" setting. This should be between 140 and 150 degrees Fahrenheit (60 to 66 degrees Celsius).

3 Line a cookie sheet with microwave-safe plastic wrap. Then spray lightly with cooking spray.

4 Spread the pear-flavored applesauce in a thin layer across the baking sheet. Use a spoon to add the blueberry-flavored applesauce in diagonal lines across the baking sheet.

5 Gently tap the sheet on the counter to help the applesauce spread flat.

6 Place the tray in the oven and cook for 6 hours. The fruit leather will be slightly sticky, yet should pull easily from the plastic wrap.

7 Use a pizza cutter or clean scissors to cut the leather into long strips. Use parchment paper to roll the leather into roll-ups, and store in a plastic bag.

Delaney's Raspberry Fizz

Delaney bribes her friends for help with a promise of special slushies. Raspberry fizzes are the perfect after-audition drink, no matter who wins the role of the Mad Hatter.

WHAT YOU'LL NEED

2 ounces (60 grams) pineapple juice

1 small scoop raspberry sorbet

½ cup (120 mL) ice cubes

6 ounces (165 grams) lemon-lime soda

FOR THE GARNISH

at least two different kinds of melon, such as watermelon, honeydew, or cantaloupe

flower-shaped cookie cutter

small round cookie cutter

paper straws

Toss all ingredients in a blender and pulse until combined. Garnish with melon flowers (instructions below).

1. With an adult's help, cut the melon into slices at least 0.5 inch (1.3 centimeters) thick.
2. Use the flower-shaped cookie cutter to cut flower shapes out of the slices.
3. Use the round cookie cutter to cut out the center of each flower.
4. Switch melon centers. For example, give a watermelon flower a muskmelon center, and vice versa.

5. Insert a toothpick into a flower, and use to garnish each fizz.

Creative Juices' Pumpkin Swirls

Willow's parents own a smoothie store called Creative Juices. She always has the latest, greatest frozen concoctions to share at sleepovers!

WHAT YOU'LL NEED

- 1 cup (240 mL) canned pumpkin
- 1 cup plain yogurt
- ½ teaspoon (2.5 mL) cinnamon
- ½ teaspoon ginger
- ½ teaspoon nutmeg
- ½ teaspoon vanilla
- 2 teaspoons (10 mL) brown sugar
- 8 ice cubes
- whipped topping
- molasses (optional)

1. Place pumpkin, yogurt, spices, vanilla, and brown sugar in a blender.

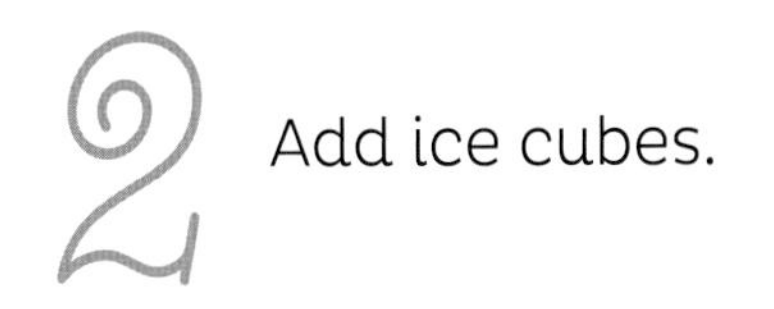

2. Add ice cubes.

3. Put the cover on the blender. Using the blender's puree setting, combine ingredients until smooth.

4. Pour equal amounts of smoothie into the glasses.

5. Decorate with whipped topping. Sprinkle additional cinnamon and nutmeg over the top.

Maren's Wake-Up Call

Maren knows the best way to start the day is with the Sleepover Club and a short stack of pancakes. These fluffy, fruity flapjacks will ensure nobody oversleeps.

WHAT YOU'LL NEED

1 large egg
2 tablespoons (30 mL) olive oil
1 teaspoon (5 mL) lemon juice
½ cup (120 mL) buttermilk
1 cup (240 mL) flour
1 tablespoon (15 mL) sugar
1 tablespoon baking powder
½ teaspoon (2.5 mL) salt
2–3 tablespoons (30–45 mL) butter
½ cup fresh blueberries
⅓ cup (80 mL) ginger ale

1. Crack an egg into a mixing bowl, and throw away the shell. With a whisk, beat egg until frothy.

2. Add olive oil, lemon juice, and buttermilk to the mixing bowl. Mix ingredients together with the whisk.

3. Add flour, sugar, baking powder, and salt to the mixing bowl. Mix until just combined.

4. Place 1 tablespoon (15 mL) butter onto a griddle. Heat on medium until butter melts. Make sure the melted butter covers the entire surface of the griddle.

5. As the griddle heats, stir the blueberries and ginger ale into the batter. Pour ¼ cup (60 mL) circles of batter onto the hot griddle.

6. Let the pancakes cook for about three minutes. When bubbles form and pop on the pancakes, flip the pancakes over with a spatula. Cook for three more minutes and remove pancakes with the spatula. Place pancakes on a plate.

7. Repeat steps 4–6 until all the batter is gone. Serve hot with butter, syrup, or whipped cream.

Willow's Cheesy Kale Bagels

Cheesy kale bagels are Willow's signature snack. If pancakes aren't your morning go-to, give these wholesome circles a try.

WHAT YOU'LL NEED

1 tablespoon (15 mL) olive oil

1 garlic clove, minced

2 cups (480 mL) kale, cleaned and cut into small pieces

salt and pepper, to taste

½ cup (120 mL) shredded cheddar cheese

1 block low-fat cream cheese

1 whole wheat bagel

1 whole garlic clove

1. In a small pan, sauté garlic in olive oil until softened, about two minutes.

2. Add kale, salt, and pepper. Sauté for another two minutes or until kale is wilted. Let cool completely.

3. Mix kale mixture, cheddar cheese, and cream cheese in a food processor until well combined.

4. Cut bagel in half and toast. Rub the inside of each bagel half with a garlic clove.

5. Spread bagel with cream cheese mixture, and serve.

Sleepover Club Caesar

Caesar salad has never been easier with this quick recipe. All you need is a food processor or a blender. You'll have enough for a Sleepover Girl-sized salad in minutes.

WHAT YOU'LL NEED

2 garlic cloves

¼ cup (60 mL) white vinegar

1 teaspoon (5 mL) Dijon mustard

3 tablespoons (45 mL) lemon juice

1 teaspoon (5 mL) sugar

¼ cup (60 mL) olive oil

salt and pepper, to taste

1 tablespoon (15 mL) Parmesan cheese, plus more for topping

Romaine lettuce

croutons

cherry tomatoes, quartered

1 Place garlic in a food processor or blender and chop finely.

2 Add vinegar, mustard, lemon juice, and sugar. Blend well.

3 Add olive oil, salt and pepper, and Parmesan cheese. Blend until everything is combined.

4 Pour over lettuce, and toss until lettuce is thoroughly coated. Top with croutons, cherry tomato pieces, and more Parmesan cheese.

TIP: For truly authentic Caesar salad, add 1 teaspoon of anchovy paste to the garlic.

Tommy D's Hot Wing Sliders

Maren's favorite pop star, Luke Lewis, is a Valley View native. Burgers are what he orders at his hometown haunt, Tommy D's. Luke himself would give these turkey sliders his seal of approval.

WHAT YOU'LL NEED

1 pound (455 grams) ground turkey

1 ½ teaspoons (7.5 mL) hot pepper sauce

2 teaspoons (10 mL) honey

1 teaspoon (5 mL) red wine vinegar

½ teaspoon (2.5 mL) smoked paprika

½ teaspoon black pepper

3 tablespoons (45 mL) plain bread crumbs

cooking spray

prepared cole slaw

8 slider buns

1. Place the ground turkey in a mixing bowl. Add the hot sauce, honey, vinegar, paprika, pepper, and bread crumbs.
2. Mix well with your hands. Form into eight flat, round patties, about 2 ounces (55 grams) each.
3. Spray the grates of the gas grill with cooking spray. Have an adult preheat the grill on high for about five minutes. (If you don't have a grill, use a stovetop frying pan.)
4. With an adult's help, lay the patties on the grill. Cook on medium heat for five minutes. Flip over with a turner. Cook for five more minutes on the other side or until the centers are well done.
5. Take the patties off the grill with a turner. Use a clean brush to top each patty with more hot sauce.
6. Place patties on the bottoms of the slider buns. Top with cole slaw and bun tops.

VEGGIES ONLY!

If you don't eat turkey, beef, or chicken, try a veggie burger. You can find them in your grocer's freezer. Make sure you buy unseasoned ones so the sauce doesn't clash. Or you can try grilling a Portobello mushroom cap. These large mushrooms are hearty alternatives to meat. Brush them with the mixture of hot sauce, honey, vinegar, paprika, and pepper before grilling.

GRILL SAFETY

Have an adult show you how to use a gas grill. Watch out for the open flame, and turn off the gas when you are done.

Ashley's Simple Spaghetti Sauce

Ashley's Italian family can make a mean bowl of spaghetti sauce! Feed a crowd—or a group of hungry Sleepover Girls!

WHAT YOU'LL NEED

1 tablespoon (15 mL) olive oil

3 garlic cloves, minced

½ cup (120 mL) onion, chopped

1 14.5-ounce (435 gram) can diced tomatoes

1 28-ounce (840 gram) can crushed tomatoes

1 6-ounce (165 gram) can tomato paste

3 tablespoons (45 mL) fresh basil (or 1 tablespoon dried basil)

pinch of sugar

1 Heat the oil in a large pot over medium heat. Add the onion and garlic. Stir until the onion starts to brown and turns transparent, about four minutes.

Add the diced tomatoes, crushed tomatoes, tomato paste, basil, and sugar. Stir well.

Bring the sauce to a boil. Then reduce heat to low. Cover the pot and simmer for about 30 minutes, stirring occasionally.

4 Serve sauce over spaghetti or your favorite noodles.

TIP: To avoid using the stove, place all ingredients in a slow cooker instead. Cover and cook on high for 8–10 hours.

Valley View Veggie Pita

Just because you're in a hurry doesn't mean you can't have a great lunch. Delaney's dad knows this, which is why he's got a mean veggie pita recipe at the ready.

WHAT YOU'LL NEED

whole cucumber

¼ cup (60 mL) chopped red onion

¼ cup sliced black olives

⅓ cup (80 mL) feta cheese, crumbled

4 teaspoons (20 mL) olive oil

1 teaspoon (5 mL) balsamic vinegar

¼ teaspoon (1.2 mL) dried oregano

pita pockets

Romaine lettuce

sliced tomatoes

1 Peel the cucumber, and chop into small pieces. Place in bowl.

Add the chopped onion, olives, and feta cheese.

In a separate bowl, combine the olive oil and vinegar. Whisk together until the liquids are no longer clear.

Pour over the cucumber mixture. Sprinkle on oregano and stir gently.

Line pita pockets with lettuce and tomatoes. Scoop in cucumber mixture.

Midnight Snack

Traditional middle-of-the-night brownies get a fresh update when turned into dessert pizza. Keep some slices on hand and your friends will be begging for you to host the next sleepover.

WHAT YOU'LL NEED

1 box brownie mix

1 8-ounce (220 gram) block cream cheese

¼ cup (60 mL) powdered sugar

1 teaspoon (5 mL) vanilla

fruit, such as blueberries, mandarin orange segments, kiwis, and strawberries

shredded coconut

chocolate syrup

1 Prepare brownie mix according to the directions on the box.

2 Press brownie mixture into a greased pizza pan. Bake at 350 degrees F (180 degrees C) for 30 minutes, or until edges are crusty.

Use oven mitts or pot holders to remove the pizza pans from the oven. Allow brownie to cool for 1 hour.

In a large bowl, combine cream cheese and powdered sugar. Use electric beaters to mix until light and fluffy.

5 Spread cream cheese mixture over the cooled brownie.

Chop strawberries and kiwis into small pieces. Top pizza with fruit and coconut. Drizzle with chocolate syrup.

Dog Days Pupcakes

Delaney loves her favorite pooch, Frisco. Create cute cupcakes to look like your best canine (or feline) friend, and host a party even a dog could love.

WHAT YOU'LL NEED

vanilla buttercream frosting (see recipe on page 31)

pink food coloring

black food coloring

cupcakes

large black jellybeans

flower-shaped sprinkles

pink taffy

blue taffy

one stick soft pink chewing gum

1 Make a double batch of vanilla buttercream. Divide most of the frosting between two bowls. Add a small amount of frosting to a third bowl.

2 Set one of the larger bowls of frosting aside. Color the other large bowl with pink food coloring. Color the small bowl with black food coloring.

3 Use a knife or an offset spatula to lightly frost the top of the cupcakes with pink frosting. (Use white if making a white poodle.)

4 Fit one piping bag with a jumbo open-star tip. Spoon in pink frosting. Use short, side-to-side motions on each side of the cupcake for ears.

TIP: Use gel food coloring, if possible. You'll need less, which means less risk of changing the flavor or texture of your icing.

continued

Move the tip in a swirl to add the fluffy hair on the top of the poodle's head. Repeat for the poodle's nose.

6 Spoon white frosting into a zip-top bag. Seal, and use scissors to cut off one corner of the bag. Use white frosting to make the poodle's eyes.

7 Press a black jellybean into the poodle's nose.

8 Spoon black frosting into a zip-top bag. Seal, and use scissors to cut off one corner of the bag. Add black dots to the center of the white eyes, and draw two curved lines for the poodle's mouth.

Add tiny white dots over the black eye dots.

10 Add a sprinkle to the poodle's ear for a bow.

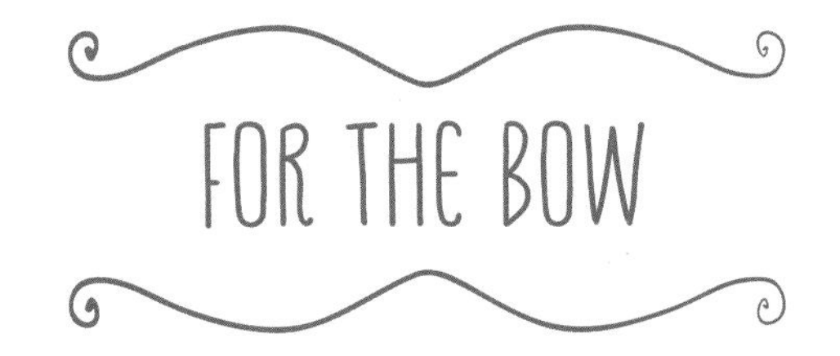

FOR THE BOW

11 Unwrap a piece of taffy and warm in your hands. Round off the corners, and pinch the middle.

12 Cut a thin strip of the chewing gum. Wrap the strip around the narrow middle of the bow. Use a toothpick to gently press the gum into the ribbon. Then press the bow onto the cupcake.

VANILLA BUTTERCREAM FROSTING

½ cup (120 mL) unsalted butter, softened
½ teaspoon (2.5 mL) vanilla extract
2 cups (480 mL) powdered sugar
1 to 2 tablespoons (15 to 30 mL) milk

1. In a large bowl, cream the butter and vanilla until fluffy.

2. Alternate adding sugar and milk until the ingredients are mixed well. The frosting should be thick, creamy, and spreadable.

NO BLACK FOOD COLORING? NO PROBLEM!

If you don't have black food coloring, try this alternative. Combine an equal amount of cocoa powder with milk, and add to frosting. Then stir in a combination of red, green, and yellow food coloring until the mixture is as dark as you want.

sleepover Girls

Paper punch-outs bring the Sleepover Girls to life! From photo frames and door hangers to bookmarks and sticker pages, you can bring Maren, Delaney, Ashley, and Willow wherever you go.

insert photo
insert photo

USE PUNCH OUT FACES TO ATTACH TO PARTY FAVORS ...

DECORATIONS, OR YOUR OWN SLEEPOVER INVITATIONS!

SHHH!
READING
HAPPENING

ENTER IF YOU
DARE

sleepover Girls
sleepover Girls

SHARE OR DARE

double shares

SHARE OR DARE

dares

SHARE OR DARE

triple dares

1. If you could only watch one TV show for the rest of the life, what would you choose?

2. What's the oldest clothing item you still wear?

3. Would you rather ride a horse or a 4-wheeler?

4. Who's your favorite fictional character, and why?

1. Pick one—never read another book, or never watch another movie.

2. What's the one thing you can't live without?

3. If you could only wear one color of nail polish for the next year, what would it be?

4. Would you rather be rescued by a policeman or a fireman?

1. Ask permission the next time you need to use the restroom.

2. Be as still as a statue for the next three turns.

3. For the next three turns, sing a TV jingle whenever someone talks to you.

4. Pretend you're swimming underwater the next time you get up and move around.

1. What's your most annoying habit?

2. If you could only pick one, what would be your super power of choice?

3. Would you rather grow your own food or make your own clothes?

4. Would you rather go without food or go without sleep?

5. Give a one-word description for each of the other players.

1. Hug the next person who walks into the room, and don't let go.

2. Do your best Tarzan yell.

3. Do a dance to the song of the other players' choice.

4. Jump in an ice-cold shower with all your clothes on.

5. Eat a serving of crackers. Then try to whistle your favorite song.

1. Let the other players do your hair.

2. No talking for the next three turns! If you have something to say, write it down.

3. Eat something without using your hands. The other players get to pick the food.

4. Record a video of you singing a popular song. For an extra dare, upload the video to YouTube.

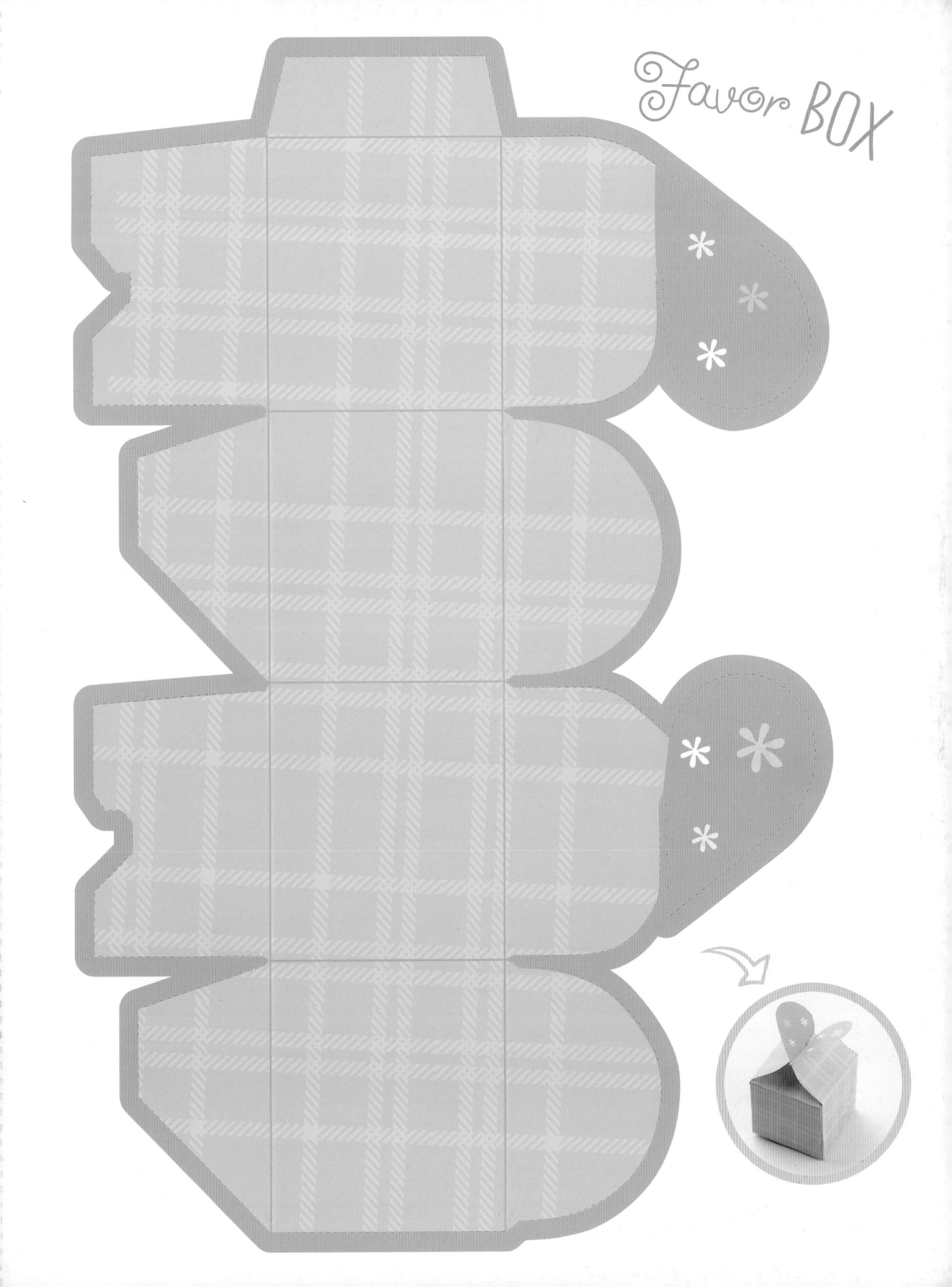
Favor BOX

You're Invited

TO A SLEEPOVER!

With: ____________________

Where: ____________________

When: ____________________

RSVP: ____________________

You're Invited

With: ____________________

Where: ____________________

When: ____________________

RSVP: ____________________

Thank You!

Thank
You!

BOOKS ARE SWEET
I READ RECIPE BOOKS
I <3 BOOKS

sleepover Girls
sleepover Girls
sleepover Girls

USE THESE STICKERS TO CUSTOMIZE FAVORS, DECORATIONS OR YOUR SLEEPOVER INVITATIONS!

Thank You!

What's Your Kitchen IQ?

The Sleepover Girls have learned a few cooking lessons the hard way (remember that whole burnt spatula in the cheese balls incident?). Could you teach them a thing or two about cooking? Test your own kitchen IQ with these 10 Q's.

1. Which of these isn't a type of herb?
   a) basil
   b) mint
   c) cinnamon
   d) cilantro

2. What does EVOO stand for?
   a) Eggs, Veggies, Onions, Oregano
   b) Endless Vinegar On the Outside
   c) Extra-Virgin Olive Oil
   d) Evenly Out of the Oven

3. All of these are things you might do to a turkey except:
   a) basting
   b) carving
   c) roasting
   d) boiling

4. Time to make some cupcakes! You'll need all of these except:
   a) muffin tin
   b) mixer
   c) thermometer
   d) spatula

5. How many teaspoons are in a tablespoon?
   a) 2
   b) 3
   c) 5
   d) 10

6. All of these are ways to cut a veggie except:
   a) piercing
   b) mincing
   c) dicing
   d) julienning

7. It's an egg-scellent morning. You're craving an egg that is fried on one side and runny on the other, called:

a) poached
b) hard-boiled
c) scrambled
d) sunny side up

8. All of these are things you might add to boiling pasta water except:

a) olive oil
b) salt
c) pasta sauce
d) none of the above

9. Which of these dishes would you make in a wok?

a) stir-fry veggies
b) cinnamon rolls
c) Italian noodles
d) veggie burgers

10. What is the proper temperature for cooked chicken?

a) 100 degrees
b) 125 degrees
c) 165 degrees
d) 195 degrees

If you got 0-2 answers right, you're a Cooking Newbie! Making your own meals? No way—you're more comfy with takeout than tackling the kitchen. And when it's time to bring homemade goodies to school, you're likely to call on Mom or Dad to make it happen. But it's never too late to learn! (Lesson #1: don't put foil in the microwave.)

If you got 3-5 answers right, you're a Future Foodie! Okay, so maybe "Top Chef" isn't must-see TV for you just yet, but that doesn't mean you're not on your way. You're still getting to know the kitchen and learning how to make simple recipes. With a little more hard work, you'll have something on the table in no time.

If you got 6-8 answers right, you're a Chef in the Making! Odds are that when your parents are making dinner, you're right there by their side soaking it all in. And that's the makings of a soon-to-be sous chef! Keep learning and observing, and you're sure to succeed.

If you got 9-10 answers right, you're a Kitchen Whiz! Foodie fun is what you're all about, and your friends and family can't wait to see what you'll whip up next. You learned how to cook at a young age and now you've turned into quite the culinary cutie!

answers: 1. c 2. c 3. d 4. c 5. b 6. a 7. d 8. c 9. b 10. c

MAD LIB

Dinner time!

And Willow knew just what she wanted to make:

_______________ _______________ _______________.
[adjective] [color] [type of food]

The first ingredient she needed was _______________, but it was
[type of spice]

way up on the top pantry shelf, so she recruited her twin Winston

to help her get it down. "You're lucky I've got long arms," joked

Winston, pretending to wind up like _______________ and throw it to
[baseball player]

her. Willow stuck her tongue out at him. "You're not done yet," she said,

handing him a _______________. "Get to work, _______________!"
[kitchen tool] [name of famous chef]

While Willow gathered the rest of the ingredients, Winston fired up

a pot of water, and soon it was bubbling like _______________.
[adjective]

They _______________, _______________ and _______________ until
[past-tense verb] [past-tense verb] [past-tense verb]

their creation was complete. Willow dug in with

her _______________, then handed Winston the first bite.
[kitchen utensil]

"We make a good team, just like _______________ and
[name of famous duo]

_______________," laughed Willow, as Winston grabbed
(name of other half of famous duo)

the _______________ from her and stuffed more into his
[type of food]

mouth. "Bon appetit!"

Join the fun by following Delaney, Maren, Ashley, and Willow's adventures in the Sleepover Girls series!

Then start the party with Sleepover Girls Crafts. Each book will show you how to replicate the fashions, crafts, and recipes created by the Sleepover Girls.

FUN & FABULOUS CRAFT AND ACTIVITY TITLES

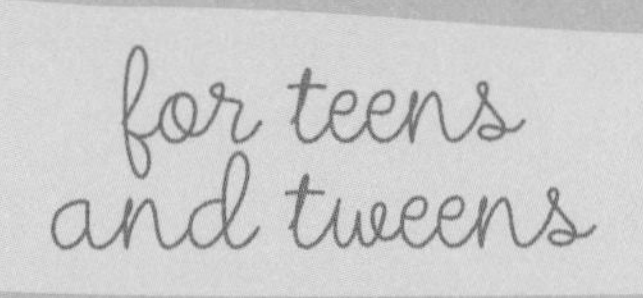

Capstone Young Readers are published by Capstone, 1710 Roe Crest Drive, North Mankato, Minnesota 56003.

www.capstoneyoungreaders.com

Library of Congress Cataloging-in-Publication Data
Cataloging-in-publication information is on file with the Library of Congress.

978-1-62370-197-0 (paperback)

Printed in China.
032014 008081RRDF14

Designer: Tracy Davies McCabe
Craft Project Creators:
Kim Braun & Marcy Morin
Photo Stylist: Sarah Schuette
Art Director: Nathan Gassman
Production Specialist: Laura Manthe

Photo Credits:
All Photos By Capstone Press: Karon Dubke

Artistic Effects:
shutterstock